NIGHTMARE IN A SEA OF MUD

NIGHTMARE
IN A SEA OF MUD

Gerald Garibaldi

Illustrated by Charles Shaw

RAINTREE PUBLISHERS
Milwaukee • Toronto • Melbourne • London

Copyright © 1980, Raintree Publishers Inc.

All rights reserved. No part of this book may be reproduced or utilized in any form or by any means, electronic or mechanical, including photocopying, recording, or by any information storage and retrieval system, without permission in writing from the Publisher. Inquiries should be addressed to Raintree Publishers Inc., 205 West Highland Avenue, Milwaukee, Wisconsin 53203.

Library of Congress Number: 79-22418

2 3 4 5 6 7 8 9 0 84 83 82 81

Printed and bound in the United States of America.

Library of Congress Cataloging in Publication Data

Garibaldi, Gerald.
    Nightmare in a sea of mud.

    SUMMARY: Describes a man's fight against waist-deep mud, snakes, crocodiles, and quicksand while trying to get help for his companions stranded in quicksand and facing slow death.
    1. Adventure and adventurers — Juvenile literature.
[1. Survival] I. Shaw, Charles, 1941-   II. Title.
G525.G364   910'.4   79-22418
ISBN 0-8172-1558-1 lib. bdg.

CONTENTS

year: 1982

Chapter I

Raintree, Inc.

CHAPTER 1

The Test Begins

When nature decides to test a man or woman, there is always danger in the testing. But danger strikes like lightning, unseen and without warning.

Usually, there is nothing in the days before, often in the very morning of the day itself, to suggest that danger is drawing near. There is nothing to point out one certain day as the day that might end a human life.

The first rays of morning found Dennis Brown awake in bed. It was too hot to sleep. Too humid. It seemed like any other summer day in Australia. But this day was to be different. Although he could not suspect it at the time, Dennis Brown's great test at the hands of nature would begin that day. Right now, though, Dennis was thinking about the trip he had to make today, 160 miles south to Mount Isa. He couldn't wait any longer. The yearly monsoon rains had already begun.

Dennis's small cattle ranch in Australia lay just south of the great tropical forest below the Gulf of Carpentaria. It was near a small community called Frenchman's Gardens. The monsoons were heavy rains that came during the Australian summer, which lasts from about Christmas to March. And when the monsoons come, the treacherous floodwaters they cause can often maroon people in the wild outback regions for months at a time.

Frenchman's Gardens is wild and green. Hundreds of different kinds of orchids and wild flowers grow in the open meadows and in the bogs. They sweeten the air with their perfume. Parakeets and many other birds with strange sounding names flutter and call in the branches of the eucalyptus and acacia trees. Crocodiles, hidden in the mossy swamp water like logs, yawn at the sun.

The night before, Dennis Brown had packed his things into his old truck. If any sense of danger whispered to him to bring extra food, he failed to hear it.

The next morning he dressed quickly and got ready for his trip. Outside, the air was thick. Dennis could already feel his shirt sticking to his back. It meant rain was coming. There was a slight breeze. With a small sigh of relief he saw that, except for a few small clouds, the sky was clear.

He stepped off the porch toward the truck. During the night something had crawled over the hood of the truck. Whatever it was had left a trail of muddy paw prints. Dennis checked the oil and water in the truck, kicked the tires a few times, and then wiped the windshield clean.

Mount Isa, tucked away atop the rough red Selwyn mountain range, is an old copper and uranium town. It overlooks the swampy plains of the Gulf of Carpentaria to the north and the dry desert lands of the Great Artisian Basin to the south. The town and the people are like an old American western frontier town, complete with cowboys and rodeos. With Camooweal, another Selwyn mountain town to the west, Mount Isa stands as the last outpost of civilization in a 100-mile radius. It is 100 miles of jungle, swamps, snakes, and other dangerous animals. And it was never more deadly than during the monsoon rains.

Dennis enjoyed his visits to the outback, as the wilderness land in Australia is called. But all he could think of now was getting back home to his family and friends.

He guided the truck carefully along the narrow bumpy trail that led to the main road. The ground was soggy. Occasionally, he could feel the tires slip in the small puddles that had formed during the night.

The sun, an orange ball, was rising fast. Den-

nis watched it flicker through the trees. Soon the midday heat would begin. He opened the window of his truck so the wind could blow in. On the horizon, he noticed that a few more clouds had formed. They were still too few and too far away, he knew, to be of any danger.

After about four hours, he pulled the truck over to the side of the road for a break. Now the sun was high and the day was hot. He took a long drink from his canteen. Then he pulled a small piece of dry meat out of his knapsack to lunch on. He stepped out of the truck to stretch his legs. About twenty feet away a colony of white ants was dragging its morning food home. The ants build enormous hills, sometimes three or four feet tall, all across the countryside. Their bite is painful, and Dennis kept his distance. He finished lunch and drove off again.

By the eighth hour he had made good progress. The countryside had lost its orange midday tint.

It had taken on the lemon yellow colors of late afternoon. Dennis was reaching for the canteen again when he heard a thundering groan, and then the truck suddenly came to a halt. Dennis was slammed into the steering wheel, which nearly knocked him out. His lip was bleeding and he could feel a sharp pain in his shoulder.

As his head cleared, he thought he must have

hit something, something big. The gas pedal was stuck and the engine was racing. He unjammed the gas pedal and turned off the engine. Then he peered out over the steering wheel. He couldn't see anything before him on the road and there was nothing behind him. It was as if a spirit had stopped the truck.

Fear welled up inside of him. He slowly opened the door and stepped out. But he couldn't feel the ground! He quickly found himself sinking in a pool of black mud. Dennis struggled to free himself as the mud pulled him deeper. Its thick sliminess made it difficult to move. But slowly he was able to push himself away from the truck. There the ground was harder, and he lifted himself out. The road had broken open like a piece of thin ice, revealing a bottomless pocket of mud beneath. These soft pockets are common in the swampy outback, and very dangerous. They form when walls of hard rock far below the surface trap water and sand, forming treacherous wells. The sun bakes the top layer into a thin brittle skin. Sometimes the skin is strong enough to hold a thousand pounds. But other times, it can crack under the weight of a rabbit.

The front tires of the truck had sunk deep into the mud pit. The ground behind was beginning to crumble and collapse. Dennis had to work fast. His great test by the forces of nature had already begun.

Caught in the Mud

Dennis thought he might be able to build the ground up beneath the truck, and then back it out. Near a fallen acacia tree, he found a large number of thick branches and rocks. Before moving them he kicked each one. Then he carefully rolled each stone over to make sure no snakes were sleeping underneath. Wading back into the mud, he forced the branches under the front tires. The rocks were quickly swallowed by the mud.

He had been working almost two hours. His shirt was drenched in perspiration. The countryside would soon be taking on a blue color as sunset drew near. His heart pounded loudly in his chest as he climbed into the driver's seat and started the engine. It would be now or never. He held the door open and watched as he eased on the gas. The wheels began to turn. Mud sprayed everywhere. The branches started to snap loudly and twist about. He could see that the ground behind was still holding. That was good. Slowly, the truck started to move. Dennis held his breath. Inch by inch the wheels crept backward. "Come on," Dennis chanted. "You can do it. Easy. . . ."

The logs were beginning to sink fast and starting to come apart. Dennis punched the gas pedal. The truck started to slide. The wheels plunged helplessly back into the slimy blackness. Dennis's heart sank.

He turned off the engine. Then, stepping over the few scattered logs on the surface, he climbed back to the side of the road. Dennis was tired and

his shoulder had begun to ache again. It seemed that the truck had slipped even deeper into the trap. He gazed down the long, lonely stretch of road looking for help. But there was no sign of life. The jungle all around him had grown fearfully quiet, as if it were waiting and watching. The sky suddenly darkened as the shadow of a large cloud swept across the land. On the horizon, Dennis could see a black cluster of rain clouds forming.

Soon it was evening and he laid down, off the road, in a layer of tall grass. He had tried several times to free the truck. Each time he had failed. Exhausted and hungry, he watched the first star of the evening come out. The clouds on the horizon had moved closer. Crickets and frogs began to sing. The night animals were waking up to hunt the swamps for food. Dennis could feel sleep taking over his body.

While the sun was still up he had studied a map and found his position. The nearest town was Gregory Downs, a small outback settlement, nearly forty miles away. But Dennis knew he couldn't walk that far. As a boy he'd had polio. The disease had crippled him badly, and even now he walked with a painful limp.

The squeal of bats flying overhead woke him from his short nap. He couldn't sleep in the open; there were too many dangers in the night. He had to eat, too, in order to keep his strength up.

There was just enough light to make his way back to the truck.

Darkness fell quickly. The sky became almost white with stars. Dennis waited, pulling bites of dried meat from his knapsack. He kept a careful eye on the road, praying someone would pass. But few would use the road now that the monsoons were beginning.

He felt lonelier than he had ever felt in his life. Outside the truck he could hear the rustle of bushes all around him. It was too black to see. The sounds grew louder. He snapped on the headlights. On the road ahead, a pack of dingoes were suddenly frozen in the bright light. Dennis looked around. The wild dogs seemed to be everywhere, their eyes flashing wildly. Dennis sounded the horn and they scattered into the night.

Later on, he was nearly asleep when the swamp suddenly fell silent. The crickets and frogs seemed to have disappeared. Not a sound could be heard. Something was wrong. The stars, too, seemed to have vanished. The world was enveloped in darkness. Then it began to rain.

When Dennis woke up the next morning the rain had stopped. He climbed onto the hood of his truck to have a look around. The rains had come down hard during the night. In several spots the road was flooded, and deep pools of water were everywhere. He knew the Gregory

River was nearby and would soon be spilling over its banks. There were more clouds on the horizon. About thirty yards away a wild boar slushed through an open field. Mud seemed to be everywhere, as if the ground were melting.

He hoped the rain would hold off that night. As the darkness fell, he wearily climbed back to the safety of the truck and soon fell asleep.

More rain fell during the night. All afternoon the next day, the hot sun lifted the water from the ground in clouds of steam. His clothes were soaked with his own perspiration. By mid-afternoon the temperature had reached almost 105 degrees. It was hard to breathe. Most of the time, he stayed inside the cab of the truck, away from the sun's rays. There he kept a lookout.

But no one passed. By nightfall his fears began to mount. He talked aloud to himself to try and raise his spirits. He hummed songs. During the evening a lyrebird sang from a nearby tree. Dennis whistled back to it, copying its song. It kept him company late into the night, until it was finally cool enough to fall asleep.

Morning came quickly, and with it the heat of a new day. Dennis found himself growing weaker. He had eaten the last of his food the night before.

Just then, he began to hear a faint buzzing noise. At first, he thought it was just the hum of the mosquitoes, but slowly the sound became louder, closer. It was a plane! Through the windshield he saw a small search plane coming near.

The plane circled behind a clump of trees, then appeared again and flew right above Dennis, who waved and screamed wildly. It passed, and for a moment, he thought it might not have seen him. It was his only chance. But quickly the plane returned. Flying much lower this time, it shot overhead and dropped a small sack. Then the plane gained altitude and disappeared. Dennis ran for the sack. It was food! He knew the pilot would report where he was. But if help were to get there he also knew there was no time to lose. The floodwaters were rising fast. Soon no one would be able to reach him!

CHAPTER 3

Everyone Is Trapped

At the Mount Isa police station, Constable Graham Robson was watching the cluster of black clouds on the horizon. In the next room he could hear the desperate voice of a woman pleading for the rescue of her son. The woman's name was Jessie Brown.

She had rented a small plane and located her son, Dennis, early that morning. He was trapped deep in the outback. Much of the road was already flooded. Only patches of the road could be seen through the trees. At first she had thought her son's truck was only a large rock on the road. But then something caught her eye and she had immediately known it was Dennis. He was waving. He was alive. Her voice cracked with excitement and relief. "But the Gregory River is spilling over fast," she said. Even from the air she could see that its swift current had already left a trail of uprooted trees.

Constable Robson knew that stronger rains were on the way. Soon the Gregory would flatten out, covering everything for miles. Robson was an outbacker born and raised. He knew the marshland all the way up to the Gulf of Carpentaria. As Mrs. Brown described where she had found her son to Inspector Jack Vaudlin, a picture of the spot came into Robson's head. If they were ever going to reach him, they had better hurry.

The two officers decided that Robson and Sergeant Ray Brand, an older, more experienced officer, would take some food, medical supplies,

and extra road equipment to the place where Dennis Brown was stranded. A little after two o'clock that afternoon, they took off in a tough, four-wheel drive Land Rover. Although Robson could not know it at the time, he, too, would be tested by nature beginning that afternoon. And his test would be far more dangerous than even the ordeal that Dennis Brown was going through.

Slowly the truck dipped and bounded along. Brand often had to get out and go ahead on foot to lead the way. Other times he would push from behind when they ran into mud pockets or potholes. It became more and more difficult to move forward. Robson began to worry. He had not realized the road would be in such bad shape. It might be too late to reach Dennis Brown. The rain clouds were moving closer. Night would be upon them, he knew, before they could get to him.

They rounded a curve and suddenly the road disappeared beneath a vast pool of water. Robson couldn't see where the road came out again. Standing on the hood of the truck, Brand looked out over the area. Water was everywhere. It looked hopeless. Robson climbed out of the truck and sat next to Brand on the hood. They were both tired and hot, and now it looked like they might have to turn back. "We can't leave him out there, Ray," Robson said with a trace of frustration in his voice. The sun was sinking steadily. They had to choose fast. Brand agreed. "Let's go get him."

Wading carefully into the water, Brand walked along the road, testing his advance with a long stick. The truck, with Robson in it, weaved and fishtailed closely behind. They had crept along for nearly a mile when the road finally appeared again.

By nine o'clock that evening they still had seen no sign of Dennis Brown or his truck. A light rain was falling. The headlights of the truck outlined the road before them. On either side, darkness hung like a heavy curtain. Both men were near exhaustion, but there was no time to rest. They began to fear that Dennis may have been injured and was unable to signal them.

Then Brand and Robson spotted lights flashing far up ahead. They knew they had finally found him. Soon their own headlights lit up the thin figure of Dennis Brown.

As Robson and Brand climbed from their truck, spoke to Brown, and then shook his hand, he began to tremble with relief. "Thank God," he said. He was saved. Brand and Robson were glad they hadn't given up and turned back.

"We have to get out of here," Brand reminded them. "It'll really start coming down any time now." With the little strength he had left, Brown

25

helped Robson and Brand run a tow rope from the Land Rover to his truck. They worked quickly. When the rope was ready, Brand started the engine. He eased down on the gas pedal. The rope drew tight and the wheels began to spin. Little by little, Dennis's truck edged out of the mud.

"Come on," Dennis shouted. "That's it!" The rope was strong, but Brand knew a sudden jerk could snap it in two. He pushed further down on the gas pedal. The tires dug deeper into the road. Suddenly Robson noticed the ground around the Land Rover was beginning to crack. He shouted, trying to warn Brand over the scream of the engine. But before Brand knew what was happening, the road caved in. The Land Rover sunk into its own trap. Brown's truck quickly drifted back into the mud.

Now both trucks were in trouble. For the next

several hours, the three exhausted men did everything they could to release the Land Rover from the mud. But its grip was just too strong. The ground continued to crumble away, and so did their confidence.

By midnight they were completely worn out. The air was humid and hot. Dark clouds hung in the sky. The coming storm was sure to break by morning. They needed help desperately. Within

twenty-four hours they could be locked in a whirlpool of rising flood waters. Brand and Robson worked their two-way radio, trying to reach help. But the mountains that surrounded the area blocked the radio signals. The only sound they heard was static.

Robson knew that they couldn't wait. The weather was getting worse. Someone had to go for help. One of them had to hike back to Mount Isa. He offered to go, but Brown and Brand objected. They were convinced that no one could make such a trip and survive. It would be suicide. Every inch of ground would be almost impossible to move over. The river would soon cover the area. Robson could easily get lost or be attacked by any of the hundreds of deadly animals of the swamp.

But Robson knew the countryside better than anyone in Mount Isa, maybe better than anyone in the country.

After much talk, they finally agreed. That night, shortly after midnight, in pitch blackness and dead silence, Robson began his journey. His great test by the forces of nature awaited him in the black, wet and treacherous outback. Would he have attempted the journey if he knew what he would have to go through in the next few days?

CHAPTER 4

One Goes for Help

Brand and Brown watched Robson slowly disappear into the darkness. They could hear his footsteps for a while. Then they, too, faded away.

At times, Robson could hardly find his way along the road. Patches of pale starlight between the clouds lit his path a little. At night the marshland takes on an awesome appearance. Everything seems different from the daytime. The trees take on other forms. A branch becomes an evil face, a rock can look like a wild animal. Even the sounds of the swamp change. The screech of owls echoes in the blackness. The night seems to rustle and snap with a secret life.

Now, the creatures who were blind by day began to move. It was their world. Robson was an intruder.

The mud snapped loudly at his heels. For a while the noise seemed to drown out all other sounds. Robson stopped to listen. His heart was

pounding like a drum. The gray shape of a dingo rose up on the road before him. He knew others were around. He clapped his hands and the animal fled.

Dingoes were easily scared and seldom attacked people. His greatest danger was snakes. The marsh was full of them, and most were poisonous. Robson knew that the death adder and the python both hunted by night. The python grows as long as twenty-eight feet, and once trapped within its powerful coils, a person can be crushed in minutes. But it is the death adder that is the greatest danger to Australian ranchers in all the outback. Swift and silent, the poisonous death adders kill hundreds of sheep a year in the pastures.

After a couple of hours, Robson had made good progress. All around him he could hear the rush of little streams, formed by the rain, as they headed toward the Gregory River. Several times he had to wade through water waist deep. Twice he wandered away from the road and had to find his way back again.

The trail became worse. The soft ground gave way to deep muddy pockets that Robson was constantly slipping into. He chose the edge of the road to walk on because it seemed a bit firmer. Thick clumps of grass grew along the roadside, and their roots held onto the earth. At the weakest spots he used the larger bushes like river rocks, and jumped from one to the other along the road. He dared not stop to rest, or within moments he found himself sinking into the sticky mud.

Then he heard a strange sound just off the roadside. Cautiously, he stopped to identify it. It was a large animal of some kind. He was sure it had been following him. The noise continued, but the sound was covered by the thundering croak of frogs. They seemed to be everywhere. He could hear slaps as their bellies landed in the mud when they sprang away from his approach. The bushes rustled again, and Robson quickly slapped his hands together. Instantly the frogs fell silent. It was an old outback trick.

Robson listened carefully. He knew the animal was close by. He could hear it breathing. Suddenly there was a furious rustling of bushes and branches. Was it coming toward him or going away? Gradually, the sounds died out. Whatever it was had fled.

Robson sighed with relief, then went on ahead. His face was continually scratched by overhanging branches. He held his hand out in front of him to protect his eyes.

The clouds opened up briefly and stars lit the landscape. Now the going was a little easier. The hills leveled off slightly and became a meadow. A web of small creeks, formed by the runoff waters, sparkled under the starlight. He could see that they were coming together into a larger stream that ran along the side of the road. Farther ahead, he could hear the violent surge of an even larger stream. He thought at first that he must be getting near the Gregory River, but then he realized that it was still several hundred yards to the south.

A few drops of water struck his arms and face. The clouds were closing up again. He wasn't sure what he would do if it began to rain hard. He might have to turn back. He kept watching the sky. A couple of times he heard what he thought was the faint rumble of thunder far away, but the sound was too low for him to be sure.

He plowed ahead. Gradually the sound of rushing water grew louder. It seemed to be all around him. The road was full of broken branches and fallen trees. The black roots of the trees stuck out into the air like grasping hands. He sensed there was trouble up ahead.

It was quick to find him. Runoff waters had come together to form one powerful stream that now churned violently across his path. Robson could see that the road had been completely washed out for nearly thirty yards. More of the road was being pulled away every minute.

If he chanced crossing, he could easily be

swept down the stream into the jaws of the nearby river. If that happened, there was little chance for survival. Robson was afraid. He thought about all the other times he'd faced danger, but none seemed more frightening. He wanted somebody to talk to. He thought about how much he liked being alive, and he just wanted to tell that to someone.

He moved up to an inlet that looked shallow. Then he eased himself into the churning water. For a long time he simply held onto the edge of the bank. Then, taking a deep breath, he took his first steps out into the torrent. Quickly, the water was up to his chest. Often it rose up to his shoulders, but somehow he kept his balance.

The water whipped around him as he slowly tested each new step. Robson reached an underwater ledge, and the river rapidly rose up to his chin. He gasped for air. He could feel the current lifting him, pushing him further into its trap. He tried to resist, but it was too late. Within seconds he was sucked into the grasp of the swirling waters.

The surging stream swept him helplessly toward the Gregory. He thrashed at the water as hard as he could, but it held him tight. More and more shoreline whisked past, and the roar of the Gregory grew louder. Branches struck his face and arms. Then, for a moment, there was a lull in the current, and Robson was able to break free and swim to shore.

Exhausted, he crawled on his hands and knees up the slippery bank until he saw an overhanging tree branch. He reached out and grabbed onto it. Suddenly, something grabbed his arm. The branch started to move. It was not a branch at all, but a giant python! Robson yanked his arm away to free himself, jerking the snake on top of him. Both fell back and splashed, wriggling, into the stream.

CHAPTER 5

The Last Test

The weight of the snake pulled him deep under the surface of the water, and they were quickly pulled downstream. Robson fought to free himself from the snake's vicelike grip. They wrestled violently beneath the dark water. Occasionally, Robson managed to come to the surface and get a breath of air before being pulled down under again.

Suddenly he felt the snake's coils weaken. Before he could figure out what had happened, its long sleek body slipped away from him. Robson rose to the surface and looked around, but the snake was nowhere in sight. All around him he heard the deafening roar of the Gregory River. He was close to its torrent—too close. He knew now the reason for the python's retreat.

Seized with a new terror, Robson began to swim for his life. The twisting current cut close to shore, and he managed to catch the bow of a fallen tree. He pulled himself up to shore and collapsed on the ground.

After a moment, his breathing became easier, and he got to his knees. The river was only about fifty yards away. The stream had swept him far away from the road. Now he wasn't even sure which way to go. He looked around at the thick wall of jungle surrounding him. It looked impassable. Robson was exhausted. He thought about how wonderful it would be if he could just close his eyes and sleep. It was now Friday. He hadn't rested in almost twenty-four hours. The warm air felt like a blanket. "It's no good," he thought, "I can't make it. No one could make it."

Even the memory of his family and friends seemed to fade from his mind. He wondered if Dennis Brown and Ray Brand were still alive. He was just dozing off when a sudden sound shook him awake. He knew at once what the loud groan meant. It was a crocodile. Robson heard the roar again. It came from the river. Robson imagined the crocodile sniffing the water for his scent, its white mouth open in the darkness.

He had to move away from the Gregory toward the road. He pushed on, through the thick marsh. There was no trail to follow, so he had to make his own. He looked at the stars and noted the position of the Gregory River. From these, he figured out a direction that he hoped would lead him toward the settlement and the road.

Robson blindly climbed and raked his way through the thick overgrowth, never knowing what danger waited behind the next bush. Sometimes the mud reached his knees. He hadn't gone a mile when he fell to the ground again from exhaustion. "I can't get up," he mumbled. "I can't."

But something inside him kept pushing him on. He had to reach help. If he didn't get up now, Robson knew he'd never be able to get up again. Again, he forced himself to stand up and continue.

Everything seemed to be moving in slow motion. It seemed to Robson that dawn would never come. He had no idea how long he'd been walking, or how far he'd come. He wasn't sure of anything. The swamp seemed to get worse. Spiders, flies, and mosquitoes bit him savagely. Branches and thorns cut into his body.

Mechanically, he pushed one foot in front of the other over and over again, across flooded creeks and meadows. After a while he didn't even feel the stings of the insects.

Robson finally reached a patch of high ground in a clearing and stopped to rest against a tree for a moment. It was hard to breathe. The clouds opened up again, and a pale light was cast on the shadowy surroundings. Everything was still and silent. The Gregory's roar had become a soft purr in the distance. Even the sound of frogs and crickets had disappeared. The swamp had fallen into a deep slumber. Soon, it would be dawn. He had been walking for half the night. Robson looked for a landmark he could recognize, something that would tell him where he was. But nothing looked familiar. Suddenly he was afraid that he was lost.

The clouds closed up, and the air turned deathly still. Robson knew what would come soon. In the distance, the blackness was split by thin shafts of lightning. The floodwaters would soon be cascading down from the hills. A great hush closed in on him. Then the first drops of rain began to fall.

Soon, the clouds broke open and the rain swept down in blinding sheets. Robson stood still for a few moments and let the cool water wash the mud and perspiration off of him. Thunder rolled loudly overhead.

Ponds and puddles quickly formed across the trail. The landscape was turned into a vast mire of mud and pitfalls. Robson stumbled and slipped constantly. Small muddy trickles of water grew rapidly into gushing channels. The sullen mood of the swamp had abruptly changed. Robson's final test had come. But had he any strength or endurance left to face it?

Out of the Wilderness

The blackness around him slowly lightened to a dark gray. The rain had let up slightly. It was now coming down in a heavy drizzle, and felt cool on his face. He could see that his arms and legs were badly swollen, his feet caked with mud. In spite of the pain and fatigue, he was happy to be alive. Several times during the night, he thought he'd never live to see another morning. Up to now, luck had been with him. He prayed that his luck would hold out just a little longer.

For over an hour, he had been walking across a field in water up to his ankles. Hundreds of small frogs splashed playfully around his feet. Now he could see them chasing each other, hiding in the tall grass or bouncing onto water plants chasing flies. The sight of them was no comfort to Robson. He knew that hungry snakes would be stalking them.

The thick blanket of clouds overhead caught

the first rays of sunlight. The trees came alive with parrots and cockatoos. The world he knew was coming back to life.

Robson wasn't certain why he suddenly looked up, but he did. About six feet in front of him a deadly Taipan snake was facing him. The sight of the enormous reptile stopped him dead in his tracks. Its long brown body was already in a striking position. Its nervous tongue licked the air for his scent. Its angry eyes were fixed on him, unmoving.

Also known as the Brown snake, the Taipan is the most feared killer in all the outback. There is enough poison in just one bite to kill 200 sheep.

Its attack is swift and sure, and it usually bites a person in several places.

If Robson moved now, he knew he wouldn't stand a chance. The snake's long body swayed slowly. It seemed to be studying him. Waiting. Robson's body trembled with exhaustion. His knees felt like they were going to buckle. "Go ahead," he thought, "strike me. I'm too tired to fight. I don't care." He had fought the jungle all through the long night, and now it could defeat him.

Robson and the snake stood still, eyeing one another, for what felt like an hour. Then the glint in the animal's eye dulled, as if it had heard Robson's plea and taken pity on him. Slowly it lowered its head. Then it slithered into the water.

Robson remained still for a long time. Then his body relaxed and he fell to his knees. "Thank you," he muttered over and over to himself. For the first time, he felt he understood the swamp. The snake was only trying to protect itself, to survive—just as he was. The wilderness is not evil. It is made up of millions of living things, snakes, birds, frogs, trees, all wanting to survive. It has its own order, its own justice, and it can be a friend. As the orange sunlight rose through the mist, Robson was awed by the magic and beauty of the swamp around him. For a moment it looked like a fairytale land. The nightmare had passed. Soon he would reach home.

The sun warmed up the jungle, and Robson was sure now that he had taken the right direction. But he still had to find the main road. As the heat grew, the mud that covered his body hardened and fell off in big chunks. The sun's burning rays stung his arms and legs.

Finally the road appeared, but it was difficult now for Robson to stay on his feet. He staggered on, afraid that in a short while the sun would force him to his knees. Then, in the distance, through the clouds of heat that rolled over the road, Robson saw a small shiny dot flickering on the horizon. He couldn't make it out clearly, but it was moving toward him. Slowly the flickering dot took shape. It was a truck!

He waved, and stumbled toward the vision. Seconds later, the truck came to a halt beside him. The driver jumped out and helped the weary, ragged Robson into the truck. He was saved!

The man quickly took Robson into Gregory Downs. He had traveled over forty miles of some of the roughest terrain in the world. But after only a brief rest, a little food and water, and a change of clothes, Robson got in touch with the police. A rescue squad was organized. By late afternoon, only hours after his own rescue, Robson led the caravan of trucks back into the flooded outback to Dennis Brown and Ray Brand. They reached Brand and Brown late that night, after the two had almost given up hope.

When he finally made it back to Camooweal that night, Robson collapsed into bed. He didn't wake up until halfway through the next day. As he slept, the news of his heroic trek spread across

the country. He had done what many would have thought was impossible. The Queensland Police Department gave Robson its highest medal for bravery and devotion to duty. For his gallantry in the face of danger, the Royal Humane Society of Australia awarded him its highly esteemed Silver Medal. In February of 1977, the British Humane Society presented him with the highest award for bravery in all the British Commonwealth, the Stanhope Gold Medal.

Graham Robson had faced the test that nature prepared for him, and he had won. He had come through his ordeal alive. He gained a new appreciation of the wilderness and its creatures. This, and the thanks of the two men he had saved, meant more to him than the recognition of an admiring—and amazed—world.